ROBERT GODDARD

DISCOVER THE LIFE OF AN INVENTOR

Don McLeese

Rourke Publishing LLC
Vero Beach, Florida 32964

www.rourkepublishing.com

PHOTO CREDITS: Pg 7 from the Library of Congress; All other images from NASA

Title page: *About 1930, Goddard towed his rocket to its launch pad.*

Library of Congress Cataloging-in-Publication Data

McLeese, Don.
  Robert Goddard / Don McLeese.
     p. cm. -- (Discover the life of an inventor II)
  Includes bibliographical references and index.
  ISBN 1-59515-435-3 (hardcover)
  1. Goddard, Robert Hutchings, 1882-1945--Juvenile literature. 2.
Rocketry--United States--Biography--Juvenile literature. I. Title.
  TL781.85.G6M35 2006
  629.4'092--dc22

                              2005011435

Printed in the USA

Rourke Publishing
1-800-394-7055
www.rourkepublishing.com
sales@rourkepublishing.com
Post Office Box 3328, Vero Beach, FL 32964

TABLE OF CONTENTS

ROCKET MAN

When Robert Goddard was a boy in the 1880s and 1890s, life was very different. There were no airplanes in the sky. It was a time when many people still traveled by horse and buggy. But, even then, Robert was already thinking about inventing a **rocket** that could help people fly into outer space. When he grew up, that's just what he did!

Goddard working on his rocket

A BOY WHO LOVED SCIENCE

Robert Hutchings Goddard was born in Worcester, Massachusetts, on October 5, 1882. The next year, his family moved to Boston. They lived there until he was 15.

Robert was interested in how things worked. He wanted to know all about electricity and other forms of power. He loved science. He did experiments with fire, and these scared his mother.

A scene in Boston during the time Goddard lived there

THE VISION IN THE CHERRY TREE

One day when he was 17, Robert climbed a tall cherry tree. When he got toward the top, he had what he called a **vision**. In his vision, Robert looked to the sky and imagined a rocket that could fly people to Mars. He later said that climbing that tree changed his life.

Goddard's childhood visions later became a reality when the Hubble Telescope took pictures of the surface of Mars.

A SICKLY YOUNGSTER

Robert was sick very often when he was a boy. He had to miss school. He didn't finish high school until he was 21. But when he was at home in bed, he did a lot of reading. He liked what is now called science fiction. Robert especially liked stories about the amazing things that would happen in the future. He read a couple of books about flying to the moon. He wanted to do that, too!

Goddard with a vacuum tube apparatus he built for research.

THE STUDENT BECOMES A TEACHER

Even though he missed a lot of school, Robert was very smart. In 1908, he went to college. He studied a branch of **science** called **physics** at Clark University in Worcester, Massachusetts. He graduated in 1911 and soon became a teacher of physics at Clark.

Goddard taught physics at Clark University.

MO
limit of balloon, 20 miles
limit of atmosphere
200 miles
6 miles
ARTH
1 lb
solis

INVENTING THE ROCKET

In 1914, Robert started to **experiment** with how to build a rocket with an engine powered by liquid **fuel**. It would fly faster and higher than anyone thought possible.

The same explosive power that sent a rocket into space could be used in a weapon. In 1918, Robert showed the army an **invention** that he called his "rocket weapon."

Goddard stands beside his liquid-fueled rocket.

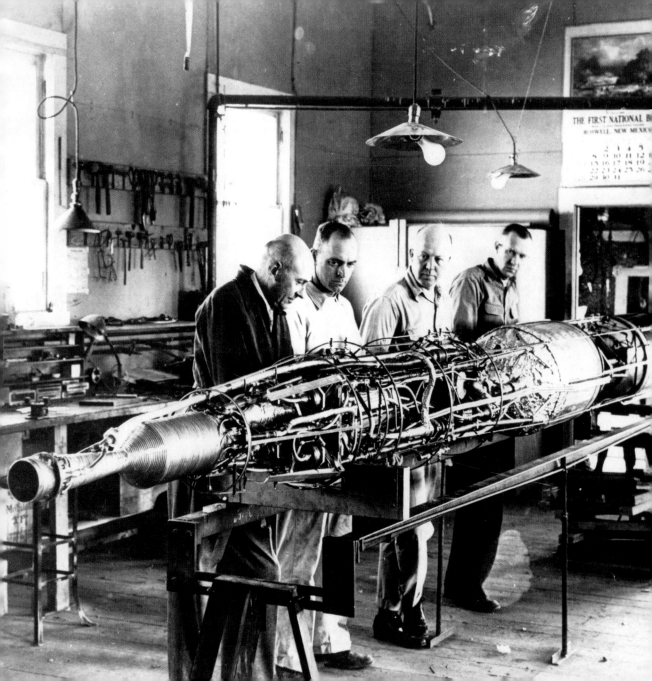

AHEAD OF HIS TIME

Robert was ahead of his time. It took the world years to catch up with him. When he started to experiment with rockets, people laughed at the idea. But Robert continued to experiment for more than 20 years.

Goddard (at left) and scientists work on a new rocket design.

THE FIRST TO MAKE A ROCKET

In 1935, Goddard was the first to make a rocket travel faster than the speed of sound. Two years later, one of his rockets went 9,000 feet (2,743 meters) into the air, the highest he ever sent one.

Standing next to the firing control panel, Goddard observes the rocket's launch site.

MAN ON THE MOON

Goddard didn't live long enough to see his rockets fly people into space. He died on April 10, 1945. But it was his rocket invention that made it possible for space exploration.

In 1969, an American **astronaut** named Neil Armstrong became the first to walk on the moon. He couldn't have done it without Robert Goddard and his rockets. Today, we remember Robert Goddard as a great inventor. He was the rocket man who brought the world into the space age.

The famous photo of Neil Armstrong on the moon in 1969

IMPORTANT DATES TO REMEMBER

1882	Robert Hutchings Goddard is born
1908	Robert goes to Clark University to study science
1911	Robert graduates from Clark and soon starts to teach physics
1914	Robert begins to experiment with a rocket powered by liquid fuel
1918	Robert shows the army his "rocket weapon"
1935	Robert invents a rocket that goes faster than the speed of sound
1937	Robert sends a rocket 9,000 feet (2,743 meters) in the air
1945	Robert Goddard dies
1969	The first American astronaut walks on the moon

GLOSSARY

astronaut (AS truh NOT) — someone who flies into space

experiment (ek SPARE uh ment) — a test of something; to try something out

fuel (FYU ul) — something that produces energy and power, like gasoline

invention (in VEN shun) — something new, developed from experiments

physics (FIZ icks) — the science of energy and physical matter

rocket (ROCK ut) — something with a powerful engine that makes it fly high and (or) fast.

science (SI entz) — what we know about nature and the way it works

vision (VIZH un) — something that you see (or think you see)

INDEX

Further Reading

Bankston, John. *Robert Goddard and the Liquid Rocket Engine.* Mitchell Lane, 2001
Roberts, Russell. *Robert Goddard.* Mitchell Lane, 2004

Websites to Visit

http://www.clarku.edu/offices/library/archives/GoddardFAQ.htm
http://inventors.about.com/library/inventors/blgoddard.htm

About the Author

Don McLeese is an associate professor of journalism at the University of Iowa. He has won many awards for his journalism, and his work has appeared in numerous newspapers and magazines. He has written many books for young readers. He lives with his wife and two daughters in West Des Moines, Iowa.